A Voice of Visions

A Voice of Visions

POETIC MEDITATIONS

⤙

Christine Kohler

FOREWORD BY *Tim D. Ware*

RESOURCE *Publications* • Eugene, Oregon

A VOICE OF VISIONS
Poetic Meditations

Copyright © 2026 Christine Kohler. All rights reserved. Except for brief quotations in critical publications or reviews, no part of this book may be reproduced in any manner without prior written permission from the publisher. Write: Permissions, Wipf and Stock Publishers, 199 W. 8th Ave., Suite 3, Eugene, OR 97401.

Resource Publications
An Imprint of Wipf and Stock Publishers
199 W. 8th Ave., Suite 3
Eugene, OR 97401

www.wipfandstock.com

PAPERBACK ISBN: 979-8-3852-7035-4
HARDCOVER ISBN: 979-8-3852-7036-1
EBOOK ISBN: 979-8-3852-7037-8

To Dr. Anthony Lee, my neurosurgeon, for his compassion as well as his skill. And to neurosurgeons and medical staff everywhere who treat people with brain tumors, brain traumas, and strokes.

To my husband, Mike Kohler, who has been my helpmate in all things.

To the Great Physician, who was gracious through every detail.

And the LORD answered me and said:
"Write the vision; make it plain . . . " Hab 2:2 (NRSV)

Contents

Foreword by Tim D. Ware | xi
Acknowledgments | xv
List of Abbreviations | xvii
Preface | xix
Introduction | xxi

After Brain Surgery | 1

Heavenly Hosts (Haiku) | 3
Ezek 1

Did Ezekiel Wake Up Screaming? (Sestina) | 4
Ezek

Be Still | 6
Ps 46:10

Vision One: the History of Mankind | 7

Battle Cry (Haiku) | 9
Josh 6

Gideon's Faith Falters | 10
Judg 6–8

The Standing Stone (Haiku) | 12
Exod 24:4; Josh 4:2–3, 24:27

Contents

Prophetic Dreams of the Unrighteous (Villanelle) | 13
Matt 5:45; Joel 2:28; Acts 2:17; Gen 40–41; Dan 2; Matt 27:19

Daniel Knows Who Holds the Key | 14
Dan 2

Vision Two: Tunnel Vision | 16

The Prophet Ate Bitter Words (Haiku) | 18
Ezek 2:8–10, 3:1–3

Prophets Invented Performance Art | 19
Isa 20:2–3; Jer 27; Hos; Ezek 4

Vision Three: God Appears in a Cloud | 20

Hypocrite, O Mighty Saul | 21
I Sam 28:3–25

Vision Four: Primordial Garden of Eden | 24

It is Not Easy Being a Prophet | 25
Jer; Dan 6:16–23; I Kgs 19:3; Isa; Matt 14:1–12; Mark 6:14–29; Rev 1:9

Vision Five: Ocean Floor | 27

Isaiah and the Seraphim | 28
Isa 6:2–7

Vision Six: Shadow Play | 31

The Silver Cord is Shattered (Sestina) | 32
Eccl 12:5–7

Vision Seven: Pre-Adamic Eden | 34

Contents

Voices Crying in the Wilderness (Sestina) | 35
Gen 21:14-21; Ps 107:4; Exod 2-3; Num 24:1-4; I Kgs 19; John 1:23; Matt 4:1-12

Vision Eight: Last Night in Eden | 37

Our Ladies of Sorrows | 39
Gen 1-4; Matt; Mark; Luke; John

John the Baptist Cries for a Sign | 41
Luke 1:5-25, 7:19-20; Matt 11:1-19; Mark 6:14-16

Transfiguration (Sestina) | 42
Matt 17

Three Cups, Two Robes, Two Crosses | 44
Matt 27-28; Mark 15-16; Luke 23-24; John 19-20; Rev 17:14, 19:16

What is the Measure of Man? | 45
Matt 25:40

Living Holy Ghost | 46
Matt 14:22-33; Mark 6:45-51

Pentecost (Haiku) | 48
Acts 2

The Light | 49
Acts 7:57-60, 8:1, 9:1-19

Seek Not Visions | 51
Deut 4; I Cor 13

Cornelius and Peter's Visions and Missions (Villanelle) | 53
Acts 10

Contents

Gold Vials of Prayer | 54
Matt 6:9–13; Rev 5:8

The Maid | 57

The Trumpet Sounds | 60
I Thess 4:16–17

Four Horsemen of the Apocalypse | 62
Rev 5:6:1–8

Elegy to the Martyrs | 65
Rev 6:9–11

No End or Beginning | 67
Rev 21–22; Gen 1:1–3

Foreword
by Tim D. Ware

PROPHETS AND PROPHECY ARE some of the most controversial and difficult passages to interpret in all of scripture. From the first prophecy in the Garden of Eden to the end of John's revelation, there is a mystery to the prophetic ministry. Pastors, preachers, and scholars have wrestled for generations to understand the people and their words.

The prophets themselves represent the breadth and beauty of God's work in and through humanity. The biblical story shows us how the Lord's prophetic gift can flow through those who never sit in the office of the prophet. The fathers of the faith, Abraham and Moses, experienced prophetic moments. Prophetic messages came through the kings Saul, David, and Solomon. The Lord used the educated, like Zechariah, along with the less educated shepherd Amos. The prophets came from all walks of life, including a fisherman who became a disciple.

A study of the prophetic context broadens the mystery and glory beyond simply looking at the people. Jeremiah prophesied amid persecution. Nathan, Ezekiel, Elisha, Isaiah, and more prophesied while also advising kings. Ezekiel and Daniel prophesied while in exile. Haggai prophesied among the remnant.

The context of who, when, and where is at the center of the exegesis process we are taught in seminary. Unfortunately, the available information is not equal. Historical and biblical data abounds for

Foreword

David, Isaiah, and John. Simultaneously, all we know about Agabus comes from a single sentence in Acts 21. This wide range creates considerable conjecture and inference in understanding both biblical prophecy and the operation of the New Testament gift of prophecy.

When we consider the prophets and the gift of prophecy, as admonished by Paul in Rom 12, 1 Cor 12–14, and Eph 4, so many questions arise. Why would God allow Saul to prophesy while trying to kill David? Why did the Lord not protect Jeremiah? Why did the Lord choose to use the real-life examples from the lives of Ezekiel and Hosea? Is all prophecy foretelling? How do we know if a prophecy is short-term or long-term?

These questions and more have plagued humanity for centuries.

One of the great tragedies of history was the 1st-century Jewish leaders' inability to see Jesus, the messiah, in the prophecies of Ps 22 and Isa 53. Still, this communicates to us the difficulty of interpreting and discerning the prophetic writings of the Bible.

Joel's prophecy fulfilled on the Day of Pentecost gives us real help in understanding prophecy. In Acts 2:16, Peter says, "This is what was spoken through the prophet Joel..." (NAB). Prophecy finds its most tremendous significance and power in its fulfillment when it moves from the prophetic to the testimony of God's omniscience.

The journey to said fulfillment is one of faith. Faith that the Lord's words are true. Faith that the Lord has a plan. Faith that the Lord is still working. Even the belief in prophecies, mysterious and incomplete, is rooted in faith.

Jesus said He is looking for faith (Luke 18:8). The book of Hebrews says faith is how we please God (Heb 11:6). The prophet Habakkuk even says the righteous live by faith.

Everything always leads back to faith in the Lord, even prophecy. Are the prophecies of God true? Will the unfulfilled word of the Lord come to pass? Can we trust the prophetic gift from the Holy

Foreword

Spirit when it manifests today? To answer each of these questions, we must look to faith.

A Voice of Visions: Poetic Meditations offers a fresh perspective on biblical prophecies and the people who delivered them. It adds to our repertoire in discerning and understanding them through a poetic interpretation of the people and circumstances. Christine Kohler's writing also reminds us this walk of faith has surrounded the prophets and prophecies from the beginning. The men and women of the past struggled through life as we do. Their words, which echo of things complete and incomplete, were given from a place of faith and confidence in the Lord. They spoke in faith that did not need to see the Son of David born of a virgin. David sang in faith, without having witnessed the Savior crucified. They shared redemption in faith without seeing the return from exile. They declared rapture in faith with centuries to wait. The 21st-century church can find in *A Voice of Visions* confidence in the prophetic gift and the works of God, as it reminds us Jesus uses broken vessels to proclaim his truth in the seen and unseen.

Tim D. Ware, MA, former missionary, church consultant, current lead pastor at Crossing Place Church, Granbury, Texas.

Acknowledgements

I BELIEVE IN GIVING honor where honor is due. My heart is full of gratitude to Wipf and Stock for selecting *A Voice of Visions: Poetic Meditations* to publish. Kudos to Managing Editor Matthew Wimer for guiding me through this process. And a hearty thanks to Joe Dehlanty, the marketing director.

My husband Mike, who claims poetry is his least favorite genre, was a patient listener, a wonderful critic, and copy editor. I am grateful to author Doris Holik Kelly who heard many of these poems in first draft. I appreciate your friendship, Doris. I also want to acknowledge Dr. Jennifer Sherman—an outstanding poet and professor—for squeezing my book into her demanding schedule and copy editing *A Voice of Visions*.

Credit goes to Lisa Bell, editor, for publishing "The Silver Cord is Shattered" in the 2025 anthology *Memories and Revelations* (Radical Women).

Abbreviations

Genesis	Gen
Exodus	Exod
Numbers	Num
Deuteronomy	Deut
Joshua	Josh
Judges	Judg
1 Samuel	1 Sam
1 Kings	1 Kgs
Nehemiah	Neh
Psalms	Ps
Ecclesiastes	Eccl
Isaiah	Isa
Jeremiah	Jer
Ezekiel	Ezek
Daniel	Dan
Hosea	Hos
Joel	Joel
Habakkuk	Hab
Matthew	Matt
Mark	Mark
Luke	Luke
John	John
Acts	Acts
Romans	Rom
1 Corinthians	1 Cor
Ephesians	Eph

Abbreviations

1 Thessalonians	1 Thess
Hebrews	Heb
New American Bible	NAB
New Revised Standard Version	NRSV

Preface

WRITERS WRITE TO SORT puzzles out. On July 31, 2024, Dr. Anthony Lee, a neurosurgeon, performed a craniology and removed a benign tumor the size of a golf ball from my brain. Two days later, after I was released from ICU, I had visions for four days and four nights. The visions came every time I closed my eyes. They were incredible, spiritual, and realistic, as if I was there in the vision. The last two nights at home I wrote about the visions. Then I begged God to make them stop and let me sleep.

Several years before brain surgery I had night terrors. (I still get them.) After several nights of night terrors I wrote a sestina, "Did Ezekiel Wake Up Screaming?" Prior to this, when I read about visions and prophecies in the Bible I only focused on trying to make sense of what they meant. After I wrote the sestina, my focus shifted to wondering what the people in the Bible felt like and thought about concerning spiritual phenomena they encountered.

After the post-surgery visions, I turned again to poetry to try to make sense of my own experiences and tell about the visions, both mine and those in the Bible. I focused on the people and not the meanings behind the prophesies. There was good reason for angels throughout history to say, "Fear not," when supernatural beings visually appeared. Imagine seeing seraphim with six wings beside a throne in heaven. The heavenly beings chant, "Holy, holy, holy," to the rhythm of their wings fanning God. What must men like Isaiah, Ezekiel, and John the Revelator felt? Pretty indescribable, but unforgettable. We are privileged they didn't keep the images

PREFACE

to themselves, afraid of being called crazy, and wrote the visions down the best they could, bounded by language. *A Voice of Visions: Poetic Meditations* is my humble attempt, with limited descriptors, to pay homage to these brave men and women who dared tell about spiritual visitations and visions.

Introduction

To write an exhaustive collection of poems about all visions and prophesies and paranormal phenomena in the Bible would be impossible. Instead, I wrote about what struck me, even how John the Baptist did not get a vision, or angelic visitation, or a sign while in prison.

Of the forty poems, I wrote nine in free verse about the visions I had after brain surgery. Five haikus balance the pace of this collection. Four are sestinas—two Old Testament and two New Testament. Two poems are Villanelles, and the rest are free verse.

Besides the biblical theme of visions, prophets, and spiritual phenomena, in the last half of the collection are several poems about the cyclical nature of man and God. We say that God is the Alpha and Omega, but he is actually without beginning or end. Reading the Bible in the manner I did while contemplating these poems, I could see clearly how Genesis and Revelation are like mirrors, reflecting each other in themes and spiritual beings and happenings. The threads from Genesis weave consistently throughout the entire Word. It reminded me of writing a deconstruction literary criticism of how James Joyce illustrated the cyclical nature of all things in *Finnegan's Wake*. I conveyed these ideas in poetry form.

When reading these poems, try putting yourself in the person's frame of mind. What must it have been like for Ezekiel, Daniel, Isaiah, Jeremiah, Habakkuk, John the Revelator, and dozens of other prophets, to see fantastical visions? Or for Joan of Arc, feeling the urgency to make people believe her, and fight in battle? Or

INTRODUCTION

how emotional John the Revelator must have felt to see his brother and disciple-friends in heaven after they had been martyred? My hope is that after reading *A Voice of Visions: Poetic Meditations*, you will read the scriptures with renewed vision.

After Brain Surgery

"What did they see?"
I asked the nurse days after brain surgery.
"People," she said,
and walked out of my dark hospital room.
People? Known or unknown?
Dead or alive? A zombie apocalypse,
Resurrection city, or ordinary cousins?

"What did they see?"
I asked the next nurse handing me a pill.
Mustn't let fever fill the tumor-less void.
"Butterflies." I swallowed, closed my lids
and contemplated monarchs, luna moths,
snout butterflies migrating *en masse*
over ICU beds of head trauma patients.

"What did they see?"
I asked the neurologist, no longer surprised
the question startled no one. Do all head
cases see visions after brains lay open to air?
"Spiders." He might as well said dragons,
boogey-men, bungee-jumping, or monsters.
So, this is what fear and phobias look like in 3-D.

How many neurological patients never confess—
after the blood-soaked scalpel retires,
after the skull is put back, the scalp stapled,
and morphine wears off—they see visions?
What did they see?
What did you see?
What did I see?

Let me tell you
beginning at the time of creation
before birds cawed, before animals chattered,
before man was formed from the damp red dirt.
Let me tell you
when God took me to the depth of the sea,
when he showed shadow-play in the Amazon.

I tell you truthfully.
In the beginning, there were visions . . .

Heavenly Hosts

(Haiku)

Mythical creatures
Cherubim—man, lion, ox, eagle—
bronzed in Zeke's vision

Did Ezekiel Wake Up Screaming?

(Sestina)

Did Ezekiel the prophet wake up screaming
when the heavens opened and he saw a vision?
Faces of man-lion-fox-eagle on four unique beasts,
sixteen wings, brass hooves, rings and rings of eyes all-seeing,
a wheel in a wheel. Caught in whirlwinds, lightning, fire,
Ezekiel, a watchman, sounded the warning alarm.

Did night terrors seize him after the chilling alarm?
Did the prophet, the watchman, wake up screaming?
Dizzy from spinning, sweating from flashing fire,
the nightmare did not end. God showed another vision:
Scrolls of lamentations and woe, he was seeing.
Good grief! He swallowed it like eating unclean beasts.

The scroll and smoke thick in his throat, the wings of beasts
flapped the smell of brimstone from him, sending alarm
through the marrow of his bones, then he was seeing
pestilence, famine, sword. Again, he was screaming,
crying out to God, "I beg you, take this vision
from me, Lord. Is this how the earth will end, in fire?"

God's Spirit entered him, even in the fire.
He swallowed his bitterness and faced the strange beasts.
Bolstered, Ezekiel prepared for the next vision.
 A watchman, alert on duty, sounds the alarm.
Princes clothed with desolation. People screaming,
rulers depend on prophets to be foreseeing.

Even if what Ezekial would be seeing
showed armies with torches consume the earth in fire.
The smell of smoke, intense heat, set him off screaming,
"Is there no peace? No treaty? I ask of you, beasts."
 His words met deaf ears. God's judgement called for alarm.
There was no mistake what he'd seen in the vision.

Forge a chain. Stop the bloody crimes. Form a vision
of defense against the violence you are seeing.
Shore up the storehouse. Bar the gates. Sound the alarm.
When the end comes, nothing will save the earth from fire.
Time watches for you, Unfaithful. Beware of the beasts.
Behold, the end comes. And you will wake up screaming.

This was his vision, the end of Earth by fire.

Be Still

Among the ruckus,
God said, "Be still
and know that I am God."
I vowed a day of silence.
Alone, no whirling machines,
no idle chatter.
The guilt voice in my head
would not shut up.
"Quiet!" I commanded.
"This is not idleness."
There is beauty in silence,
listening to my thoughts,
knowing who I am,
discovering the great I Am,
who stilled the waters,
who stills my ruckus soul.
Be still
and know.

Vision One: The History of Mankind

Closed my eyes in the sacred space
of the hospital room, fresh from ICU.
Visions scrolled behind my eyelids.
Scrolling, scrolling, scrolling,
I strained to read marks on clay tablets.
Sumerian? Akkadian? Hieroglyphics?
No, earlier. Hashtag-like cuneiform. Perhaps.
A proto-language, long dead and resurrected
into a thousand babbles of written words.

Scrolling, scrolling, scrolling.
I thought of linguistics, deconstructionism,
questioning of language. Why did Adam
call a roaring beast with claws and mane, a lion?
Or name the gentle, fleeced, follower, a lamb?
Who decided red means stop and green, go?
We forget language is derived from symbols.
I forgot I was prone on a hospital bed, my head
freshly stapled. My brain communicating
without speech, through mental telepathy.

I mentally ask the Logos to be my Rhema Word
and raise me from this bed. After all, only one
day prior, a neurosurgeon drilled through my skull,
popped the top like a pumpkin, scooped out the goop,
then patched it like Jack with vinegar, brown paper.
Or so the nursery rhymes mixed their metaphors.
The Rhema Word declined. I stayed at peace
with the living Logos Word speaking to my brain.

Scrolling, scrolling, scrolling, faster and faster.
Too quick to read the primitive marks on clay.
Symbols grew closer to recognizable letters.
Clay tablets metamorphosed into brass plates.
In a sudden surge the tablets, now like printing press plates, multiplied, increasing in numbers and speed.
Behind closed eyelids scrolled the symbols, letters.
Is this how Soloman derived God's wisdom?
Or what only prophets understand as visions?
"What am I seeing?" my brain asked.

"The history of mankind."

Battle Cry

(Haiku)

Sound a shofar horn
March around Jericho walls
A harlot's rope drops

Gideon's Faith Falters

Gideon, wasn't a prophet
and angel enough proof?
"Peace. Fear not.
You shall not die."

Yet, you tested Jehovah
with a fleece. Twice.
Sacrificed fluffy lamb fur.
Faith or doubt?

A prophet, an angel,
not proof enough?

Rise up, O man of God, build
an altar to Jehovah Shalom.
Flee from the caves, Gideon.
Tear down the altar of Ba'al.

Harken to the voice of God.
Recruit men who lap like dogs.
Arm 300 men of Israel
with lighted jars and sticks.

Blow the trumpets of Zion!
Stir up Midianites like hornets.
Blow the shofars of sacrifice.
Break the jars. Shine the light.

Jehovah Shalom shall rule
as King over the tribes of Israel.

Why take earrings for an ephod,
O Gideon? Why did you not
judge your covetous heart?
Did you not see the idolatry?

Was a prophet, an angel,
two fleeces not enough?

The Standing Stone

(Haiku)

Plant the Standing Stone
Witness their covenant
Make peace in the land

Prophetic Dreams of the Unrighteous
(Villanelle)

God's sun rises on the evil and good. At best,
young men see visions, Joel wrote, and old men dream dreams.
Even unrighteous men had a prophetic test.

In jail, Pharaoh's butler and baker were in quest
of Joseph revealing dreams with similar themes.
Baker would hang; Butler restored to do his best.

Disturbed dreams of cows and corn. At Pharaoh's behest
Joseph interpreted famine and plenty. "Glean
during fat years." Pharaoh said Joseph passed the test.

Troubled dreams caused King Nebuchadnezzar unrest.
Gold, silver, brass, iron, clay statue—kingdom scheme.
Through God, Daniel's interpretation was the best.

Claudia's dream warned her husband Pontius, lest
he condemn a good righteous man, the Christ, who seems
innocent. If he is God, was this dream a test?

Rain falls on just and unjust. Only God invests
prophetic dreams and interpretation he deems
wise and worthy to whomever will be the best
to act rightly. To God's glory is the dream's test.

Daniel Knows Who Holds the Key

It is one matter at night to dream a dream,
then in the clear-minded light of day to interpret.
But it is quite another matter
to interpret a dream not known.
Quite like your feet and hands are bound
behind your back, thrown into the Persian Gulf,
and told to swim or drown.
Quite another matter.
Quite impossible.

Yet, that is exactly what the king demanded.
Disturbed by his dreams, King Nebuchadnezzar II
ordered magicians, sorcerers, astrologers,
soothsayers—the wisest magi of Babylon—
to interpret his forgotten dream, not told.
No magic. No sorcery. No signs in the stars.
No man could conjure an interpretation
without knowing the dream. Quite impossible.
Yet, Daniel knew the One who holds the key.

He called his fellow Hebrew wise men
to petition God to give Daniel the dream
and interpretation. For it is God and God alone
who reveals the deep and secret things.
Only God knows what lies in darkness.
For it is the light that dwells within him.
Daniel and the Hebrews prayed for God
to unlock the hidden mysteries of dreams
and interpretations. Quite possible for God.

The four devout men kneeled and prayed.
Their lives and those of all wise men
would perish if Daniel did not return
to the palace and tell the king his dream.
Impatient hours passed. Finally, God unlocked
the secret to Daniel in a night vision.
A great image, head of gold, silver breast and arms,
brass belly and thighs, iron legs, feet of clay.
Broken iron-clay feet, chaff on harvest floors.

Daniel rushed to the palace with the interpretation.
Kingdom upon kingdom, kingdom upon kingdom.
Softer, weaker metals, progressing downward—
gold, silver, brass, iron, ending with feet of clay.
A prophecy of declining, diminishing empires,
until clay feet, clay toes, the weakest kingdom
smashed to dust, wind blowing it away.
Daniel gave God the honor and glory.
For God, and God alone, holds the key
to prophecy and interpretations.

Vision Two: Tunnel Vision

Finally, released from the hospital.
Released from temperature-taking.
Released from inedible food, from
catheters, and no showers. Released.

I can walk. I can talk. I can breathe!
Thank God for his graciousness,
goodness, and faithfulness to me.
I am thankful beyond belief. I can think.

Breathe! Released and relieved,
in the car I close my eyes to rest
on the journey home. A navigation
panel shows the way. A lighted map.

Opening my eyes reveals a black
glove compartment. No GPS icon.
Heavy eyelids droop. White and blue
lights show a bright path to travel.

A tunnel looms in front of our car,
like the scary dark Chesapeake Bay
Bridge-Tunnel connecting Virginia.
Darker, narrower. My pulse races.

Breathe! God will not let us crash.
Blackness engulfs. Hairs raise on gray
cloth like mohair. Breathe! Hairs sway
calmly as I inhale, exhale.

God's breath in me.
I am alive!
Released.
On a lighted path.

The Prophet Ate Bitter Words

(Haiku)

'Zek ate the whole scroll
lamentation, mourning, woe
honeycomb parchment

Prophets Invented Performance Art

Before streaking was popular,
Isaiah roamed Jerusalem
for three eye-popping years
completely jay-bird naked
as a form of political protest.

In the spirit of street performers,
Jeremiah, fully clothed, donned
a heavy cumbersome oxen yoke,
trod the city streets, a literal busker
metaphor of Babylonian bonds.

Hosea yoked himself in marriage
with a prostitute. Imagine life
with an unfaithful lying whore.
Poor children strapped with names
"not my people" and "not pitied."

If prophets invented performance art,
Ezekiel elevated street theater
by carving Jerusalem into a brick,
lying beside it four-hundred-thirty days.
Publicly eating bread baked over dung.

Prophets did more than foretell the future.
Pontificated as social and political activists.
Judges, jury, and, at times, executioners.
Prophets anointed and dethroned kings.
Oft reviled, never dull, wild prophetic acts.

Vision Three: God Appears in a Cloud

Relieved to be home and rest in my own bed,
I close my eyes and, like Scrooge being visited
by Christmas spirits, a brilliant white cloud appears
with the brown eyes of a weathered old man.
Wide, then squinty. Eyes peering from a cloud.
Not even Moses could look upon the face of God.
Could this be a Christophany, or the Holy Spirit?

The part of mind that bypasses knowledge, logic,
or reasoning says, "This is God." The Light
so bright and whiter than the sun. "I surrender.
I surrender all," my tumor-free brain sings.
Though I make no sound during these silent
moments in the sacred space of my head.

I longed to enter God's inner sanctuary.
Let me come by the blood of the Lamb.
Gracious Lord who is Rapha to me.
I yearned to kneel in the Holy of Holies.

The cloud ushered me into a dense jungle.
The Garden of Eden? At very least,
the heart of the Amazon in a primordial age.

Hypocrite, O Mighty Saul

Hypocrite, O mighty Saul,
king of Judah.
You purged the land, the holy land,
of witches and wizards.
Those who used familiar spirits
to conjure the dead for gain.

Yet, when you ceased to hear God's voice—
no dreams, no Urim, no word from prophets—
you sought the witch of Endor.
O, ye hypocrite.
Why was she not banished with wizards?
Why was she not executed according to the law?

O mighty Saul, do you wonder why
God had forsaken you?
Why he gave your kingdom
to your son-in-law, David?
When he hid among your enemies,
Philistines, whom you faced in battle.
David could not sing, strum the lyre
to soothe your tormenting spirit.

Faced with fear, much trembling and fear,
drove you to the witch of Endor.
You were not the only one afraid.
Despite your disguise, the witch knew
your true identity. Your hypocrisy.
Prophet Samuel told her. Summoned
from the grave, he pointed a bony
accusing finger. Hypocrite!

Saul swore an oath by God—
what right had he to invoke God's name?—
to spare the witch's life if she would conjure
the prophet Samuel on Saul's behalf.
Hypocrite! Why should even a witch trust
one who disobeyed law and God?

Necromancy, the witch performed.
An aged man in mantle ascended,
disquieted from the deepest slumber
of death. Saul bent in obeisance.
Distressed, the king cried out his complaint.
The giants lined up for battle.
God ignored Saul's plea for a prophecy.
Hypocrite! Your real enemy was God.
He left you because of disobedience.
The Lord gave your kingdom to David.
You refused to annihilate the Amaleks.
Still, Saul pressed forth and demanded
of Samuel a foretelling of the future.

The spirit supposed to be Samuel prophesied:
Israel would fall into the hands of the Philistines.
Saul and his sons soon meet their maker.
The Hebrews bore the yoke of their enemies.
And the house of Saul would fall.

Thus was the message of the prophet
who should never have been summoned.
Who should have stayed as silent
as the one true God, maker of Heaven
and Earth, and Saul, the hypocrite.

Vision Four: Primordial Garden of Eden

Deep in the heart of the jungle
light penetrates as gauzy gray
against muted black shadows.
Huge viny leaves obscured views
beyond thick trees and foliage.

No sound in the utter stillness.
No chattering of monkeys.
No cawing of parrots or macaws.
Listen. No scurrying of lizards,
beetles. No chirping of crickets,
or croaking of frogs. All is silent.

What am I to see? Why, God,
bring me here? Everywhere I look,
as far as the eye can fathom,
leaves and vines and trees.
No noise fills the lush, dense,
dewy viridescent vegetation.
Why this in my vision?

Ah, I am looking and listening
for something else, instead
of taking joy in the creation
of the plants alone.
They are enough.
Worthy of a vision.
Worthy of God's vision.

It is Not Easy Being a Prophet

Sanctified and ordained before birth.
Faithful obeisance to God in prayer.
Hunger pangs cramp the belly by fasting.
Prayer begat visions. Visions begat prophecy.
This is the making of a prophet.

Visions of flood, war, famine,
destruction, disease, desolation.
Visions in dreams.
Six-winged seraphim
and angel messengers.

Obscure symbols,
smoky secrets,
mysterious meanings
confound even the prophets,
requiring interpretations.

Prophets do not dare shrug,
scratch their puzzled heads,
do tricks like court magicians.
Or their dumbfounded heads
might be on a pike by nightfall.

It is not easy being a prophet.
Derided, disrespected, disregarded.
Jeremiah warned and lamented
Assyrian destruction of Jerusalem,
then fled to Egypt and obscurity.

Daniel thrown into the lion's den.
Elijah ran from murderous Jezebel.
Isaiah, misunderstood, sawed in half.
John the Baptist imprisoned, beheaded.
John the Revelator exiled to Patmos.

It is not easy being a prophet.
For all their warnings—
cries in the wilderness,
laments, depression, and threats—
did anyone heed? Did anyone?

Vision Five: Ocean Floor

Ocean waves danced over sea anemone.
Its graceful tentacles swayed gently
like a maestro conducting a waltz.
"Do not be afraid." Mind telepathy.
Mesmerizing rhythms we shared
as I sat on the ocean floor.

Bubbles emitted naturally,
unaided by breathing apparatus.
I'm a water baby, strong swimmer,
SCUBA diver in the Mariana trench.
Yet this was different, I breathed
like an oyster, calm as a clam.

Isaiah and the Seraphim

Visions thundered in his ears,
crashing like ocean surf.
Visions roared in his sight.
Lions pounced their prey.

Isaiah prophesied to Israelites.
They stopped up their ears.
He described coming dangers.
They refused to see warnings.

Darkness and sorrow blotted the land.
The light shuddered in heaven.

In his despair, Isaiah lifted his eyes.
Shekinah glory of God glowed.
His royal robe filled the temple,
flowing like a magnificent waterfall.

Above the throne stood seraphim.
Six wings—two like fans concealed a face.
Two wings like chaps covered his feet.
Middle wings flew like a hummingbird,
or dragonfly,
or goose.

One seraph—an angel of highest order
—called to the other celestial beings,
"Holy, holy, holy."
Cried in cadence with beating of wings.

Pillars shook. Incense smoke and scent
permeated the temple. Isaiah fell prostrate
before the Most High and Holy King.
He bowed before the terrifying seraphim.

"Holy, holy, holy." Wings beat to the Logos.
Earth quaked. Scented smoke billowed.

Isaiah clamped his mouth. Hid his face.
Swallowed his words. Kissed the dirt.
Isaiah groaned. How weak. How unclean
in the presence of almighty holy God.

No amount of sacrifice, or sin offering,
could make him worthy to his Lord.

"Holy, holy, holy," cried seraphim
in the throne room of the Most High.

"Unclean! Unclean!" Isaiah lamented
like a leper. "My eyes have seen
the King of Hosts. Woe, I am unworthy."

A seraph darted to the altar,
snatched a hot coal,
lunged toward the prophet.

Isaiah pursed his lips, locked his jaw.
The seraph thrust the burning ember,
touched the prophet's unclean lips,
singed the iniquity, purged his sin.

God himself spoke—not seraphim,
not lesser angels, nor equally terrifying
cherubim—but God, creator of all,
said to Isaiah, "Who shall I send?"

Who? Dare he answer?
The people did not listen.
They refused to see his visions.
They would not heed his warnings.

Dare he? Again?

"Holy, holy, holy," seraphim cried.
God's bright glory burned through incense.
God's presence overwhelmed the Holy of Holies.
Isaiah's blood offering burned on altar coals.

How dare he refuse.
"Send me, Lord. Send me."

Vision Six: Shadow Play

Awaking in the Amazon garden,
a thick branch of foliage covered my face
like a masquerade mask. Suffocating,
I wanted it off, though the Mardi Gras
façade did not touch my skin.
I could peep around leaves to view
the jungle. But the fauna-mask obscured
my vision. My mind asked God, "Why
the mask?" No answer, not even a still
small voice. Yet, I understood the wisdom,
accepting this was all I was allowed to see.

On God's terms, I peered through top branches,
searching the sky. Overcast and nighttime.
"Where are the stars?" Clouds shifted slightly.
Pinpricks of light speckled the sky, though no
visible constellations. From the corner of my
left eye burst two quick flashes of lightning.
Darkness descended. Bothered by the mask,
I focused on subtle light shifts in the sky,
shadow play, gentle movements in clouds,
obstructions, obfuscations of stars and moon.
I needed no explanation of how or why.
Content, I marveled at creation of the heavens.

The Silver Cord is Shattered

(Sestina)

Miraculous first breath from God, sever the cord
to begin life's journey into veiled mystery
from seed to flesh and bones. Water to earth. We change;
body, soul, spirit, our triune being is mortal.
Life struggling into never-ending circles
striving forward, a treasured prize of victory.

Scaling Everest-sized mountaintops to victory
depends upon trust and faith in a sturdy cord.
Looping from waist to higher points, in a circle
of mist veiling the peak from sky in mystery.
Dizzily realizing I am earth-born mortal.
One slip from solid rock and everything will change.

Plunging into unfathomable depths of change
beneath the seas, a SCUBA diver's victory
over breathing, like fish gills, possessing mortal
threads of air from a tank, regulator, and cord.
Making me one with sea creatures, a mystery
deep in time warps before life lands in a circle.

Dipping and yawing, the plane turns in a circle.
Finding a favorable spot, I shift and change.
Ready. Set. Jump! Gravity unravels mystery.
Free-falling to ground, letting go, taste victory.
Until I have no choice but to pull the rip cord.
A parachute safely lands this earth-bound mortal.

Miraculous last breath to God, leaving mortal
body behind. Dust to ashes. In a circle
new life sprouts again by a shattered silver cord.
We shall not all sleep, but we shall all go through change.
Death is swallowed up in glorious victory.
Behold, He shows an inscrutable mystery.

How one's spirit returns to God is mystery.
For this mortal being takes on an immortal
body with its soul. Death's sting denied victory.
Incomprehensible, a completed circle
without the tethers to Earth, no need for change
beyond, unfathomable freedom from a cord.

O, what mystery is an incorporeal cord.
Eternally, immortals remain without change,
abiding victory in Trinity circles.

Vision Seven: Pre-Adamite Eden

My vision shifted to the ground.
A heavy foliage mask disappeared.
Eyes blinked from the damp soil.
Green cat eyes. Blink. Red dirt.
Blink. The eyes morphed so quick
I doubted behind my closed lids
what I had actually seen. Blink. Blink.
Eyes in the dirt, increasingly muddier.

A man's face burbled to the surface.
Only to sink back into the morass.
It must be Adam before he was formed.
Faces of creatures, animals, mammals
pre-created from the oozing red clay.
Not formed enough to identify,
like the living letters and words
before my eyes in the first visions.

I rolled on my back, laid under a canopy
of trees, thick leaves, and vines at night.
No sounds. No touch. No taste. No smell.
I lie in the stillness of the Amazon garden
and contemplated the wonder of nature
before creatures and animals and man.
In the beginning, God created heaven and earth.
And it was good. It was all so beautiful and good.

Voices Crying in the Wilderness

(Sestina)

O, thou harsh and treacherous wilderness.
Hagar and Ishmael driven to desert
wasteland—hot, dry and devoid of water.
Food gone. Waterskins empty. Hagar prayed
to Abraham's God, then an angel's voice
promised her son hope, a well of refuge.

Murderous Moses fled, seeking refuge
like a strong gazelle in the wilderness.
An angel in a burning bush. God's voice.
Moses answered the call in the desert,
removed his shoes on holy ground and prayed.
He would lead Israelites through the water.

Balaam turned toward a place with no water,
far from the Moab king. He gained refuge.
No more Ba'al worship, or magic. He prayed
to the Hebrew's God in the wilderness.
Visions and God's Spirit in the desert
overcame Balaam as he sought God's voice.

Afraid of Jezabel, Elijah's voice,
not of God, ran and thirsted for water
in windstorms, a dry and barren desert.
Through earthquake and fire, he yearned for refuge.
God's still small voice spoke in the wilderness.
Covered in his mantle, Elijah prayed.

John, the forerunner of Christ, prayed.
Holy Ghost anointed, he was the voice
for Yahweh crying in the wilderness.
In repentance, John baptized in water
and Spirit. Like an owl, he found refuge
in the sacred seclusion of desert.

Jesus craved solitude in the desert.
Away from the demanding crowds, he prayed.
To Christ the arid land was a refuge.
A holy space where he heard Abba's voice.
A place where he fasted food and water.
He defied Satan in the wilderness.

In the desert, seek the great I Am's voice.
Follow how Christ prayed; drink living water.
Take refuge and embrace the wilderness.

Vision Eight: Last Night in Eden

Six days after brain surgery,
two days out of ICU,
four days of visions
every time I closed my eyes,
desperate for sleep.

Saturday, lying in bed
the brilliant white cloud
with the eyes of God
descended again. "Not tonight,
Lord. I would rather sleep."

Poof! The cloud disappeared.
One stray animal visited me.
What kind, I did not know.
Was this how Adam felt the first
time strange creatures with fur,
four legs, snouts, and grunts,
trotted to him, wagging tails?

I called the white furry creature
with a black nose, dog. Although
I didn't know for sure it was canine.
The being was not afraid of me,
nor did I feel scared of it. I laid
on my side very still and watched
the dog with short white hair sleep.

After a while, I turned over,
still desperate for elusive sleep.
Another creature came to me.
Again, I called it dog, though no proof
it was of that species. This animal
had either many appendages
or else there were multiple beings.

The animal's hair was long and reddish.
It came closer and sniffed my hand,
The creature could not get comfortable
because it fidgeted immensely. Exhausted,
I laid on my back under a thick canopy
of leaves, watching light and dark
shadow-play splaying across the night sky.

After that night, sweet elusive sleep
finally overcame me. Sweet sleep!
No more visions when I closed my eyes.
I have never doubted they were of God.
I marveled at all Jehovah had shown me.
Only He could give immeasurable peace.

Our Ladies of Sorrows

Oh Eve, you have been deceived.
How naïve to have believed
Old Slewfoot, Beelzebub, Satan.
You ate fruit in greed of wisdom,
when you could have received
by asking your Father during walks,
and talks in the Garden of Eden.

Banishment. For Eve and Adam.
Thistles and thorns, sin and sickness
shall be your lot in life 'til death.
Pain in childbirth for all women.
As did New Eve, a second Lady
of Sorrows, a virgin who bore a son
to bruise the head of the serpent.

The vile viper spoke to Eve—
Why was she not wary?
Was she astounded by a cherubim
brandishing a flaming sword?
At least Gabriel warned Mary,
"Fear not," complimented profusely,
then gave an annunciation most startling.

Eve had been the mother of mankind.
Mary became the mother of God's son.
Eve's disobedience caused an evil curse.
Mary's obedience birthed the Redeemer.
Eve conceived the first birth, first death.
Mary conceived the second Adam, rebirth,
death-defying resurrection, New Life.

Through one woman, mankind fell to sin.
Through one woman, God's redemption.
Yet, Eve and Mary, both Ladies of Sorrows,
their pain far beyond childbirth, their heavy
burdens of loss and sacrifice of their sons.

John the Baptist Cries for a Sign

When John the Baptist knelt in prison,
awaiting the executioner's axe,
where was his father's angel,
saying, "Fear not! Your prayer is heard."?

John trembled, left only with memories:
His cousin immersed in the Jordan.
Holy Spirt descended like a dove.
Divine voice from Heaven, "My son. . ."

John shook, recollection fading.
Where was the Holy Ghost now?
The mighty voice? Not in the dungeon.
Not in this wretched death chamber.

John prostrated on a cold prison floor.
Riddled with doubts, he cried out,
"Are you the Christ, the Chosen One?
Should we look for another Messiah?"

If John was in the likeness of Elias,
where were the prophet's visions
when his faith needed substantiation most?
Where was his father's angel?

Transfiguration

(Sestina)

Jesus and his disciples trudged toward a mountain top.
Rabboni's clothes and face shone bright with radiant light.
Peter, James and John fell to the ground in reverent bow
before Moses, Elijah, and Jesus, who all changed.
Simon Peter sought stones to build a holy altar
and worship law, prophet, messiah in their vision.

Building three tabernacles became Peter's vision.
A temple for Moses, who brought tablets from the top
of Sinai. For Elijah's fire on a wet altar.
And a place to worship Christ, the Way, the Truth, the Light.
A bright cloud overshadowed them, spoke, and Peter changed.
"I'm pleased with my son. Listen to him." Afraid, they bow.

Their Master said, "Don't be afraid." The disciples bow
to Jesus' words after the vanishing vision.
Only Jesus remained. But, the disciples had changed
within themselves as a result of their mountaintop
experience that showed them God's Son, the Light.
Jesus was the only one worthy of an altar.

Peter dropped stones he'd gathered for building three altars.
James and John raised up from holy ground where they did bow.
Jesus led them from where God spoke through a cloud of light.
Down from where Moses, Elijah stood in a vision,
Down, down, down from where the air thinned on the mountaintop.
Away from where everything for the disciples changed.

Midway, Jesus warned, "Do not tell until I am changed,
risen from the dead. A sacrificed lamb on the altar."
Peter, James and John looked back toward the mountaintop.
They asked, "The scribes said Elijah must come first and bow
to God's will, heralding the coming Messiah's vision."
Jesus said, "One has already come to show the Light."

Elijah had come? Who did Jesus say showed the Light?
Perplexed, the disciples wondered who declared this. It changed
how they saw Isaiah's prophecy with new vision.
They felt ashamed for desiring to build an altar.
They had the prophecy wrong. The one to whom to bow
and honor was not the Elijah on the mountaintop.

The one who showed the Light was John the Baptist. Altar
worship would change with Messiah revealed. All would bow.
They pondered the vision that day on the mountaintop.

Three Cups, Two Robes, Two Crowns

He drank one cup of suffering.
Guards disrobed him in shame.
Mockers pressed one crown of thorns,
Causing Him great pain.

Three cups, two robes, two crowns.
He accepted the cup of consolation.
Humbled as a man named Jesus.
Yet exalted as God, the Christ.

Three cups, two robes, two crowns.
For us, he drank the cup of salvation.
God crowns him King of kings.
His regal robe of righteousness.

What is the Measure of Man?

What is the measure of man
six feet under?
Bury a fish
in a lead-lined casket
and it cannot fertilize maize.

The after-life of creatures
feed, clothe, keep warm
beast and man.
The afterlife of man's soul
serves only himself and God.
(Unless Satan's eternal torment
awaits man's soul instead.)

What is the measure
of man?
That which endures
on Earth?

Except what he does before
his last breath
to feed, and clothe, and warm
the hearts and souls
of Mankind.

Living Holy Ghost

Rugged fisherman
rowed the boat
partway across the lake.
A terrifying storm
rocked the shallow hull.
Struck fear in the hearts
of the capable swimmers.
Thunder rolled.

Lightning flashed.
Revealing a figure
on distant wave.
Peter squinted against salt
spray, straining to see.
Storm clouds obscured
moon and stars. Boom!
Lightning lit the sky.

The specter form drew closer,
closer, through a hazy mist.
Peter wiped rain from his eyes.
"A ghost!" someone gasped.
No man could walk upon the sea.
The phantom drew closer, closer.
Peter stood against the wind.
"Lord!" he cried. "Is that you?"
"If not a Spirit, bid me come."

Jesus extended his hand.
"Be not afraid, it is I."
The haunting wind
echoed his words.
Peter, bold and brash,
stepped out onto a wave
crested beside the boat.
One step, two—eyes fixed
on the Master. Three steps—

Panic filled his vessel
as he looked at the deep
dark waters. Splash!
Submerged beneath the sea,
a solid hand—not shadow—
grasped hold and lifted Peter
into the boat. Flesh upon flesh.
Jesus, no hallucination or wraith.
Filled with the living Holy Spirit,
and, clearly, living flesh and blood.

Pentecost

(Haiku)

Tarry, Disciples
Mighty winds. Strange tongues. Arise!
Saints baptized in fire

The Light

In the beginning was the Light.
For God is Light, and energy
so bright no candle is needed
in Heaven, where light resides.

God filled Stephen with light,
and the knowledge of Christ.
Stephen, filled with wisdom and
the Holy Ghost, had light within.

The Deacon showed his light
humbly serving widows,
preaching The Way, healing,
in the name of Jesus Christ.

The light shined when Stephen
preached, his face like an angel.
"Stone him!" the priests cried.
Kill the light shining in darkness.

Stephen glimpsed a vision from
heaven. Glory. God's purest light.
Shekinah glory. Jesus beside him.
The vessel died, but his soul lives.

Stoners's coats thrown in the shadow
of a man with a murderous heart.
Saul of Tarsus applauded snuffing
out Stephen's life, ending The Way.

But Stephen's words were not null,
his light not void. God's brilliant
glory exposed Saul's dark heart.
Light engulfed him, blinding Saul,

Making him vulnerable, dependent.
The voice. Witnesses heard it. Voiced,
"I am. I am Jesus. I am the Light."
Saul walked in glorious luminous Light.

Darkness lifted. Sight restored.
God said, "Let there be light."
And for Saul, the light shone.
And it was good, eternally good.

Seek Not Visions

Be not like dervishes,
emotions spinning,
whirling up ecstasy,
chasing public adoration.
A mystic for tourists.

Seek not visions.
Seek not dream interpretations.
Seek not prophecy and grandeur.
Seek the one true God and his glory.

Yeah, Jehovah is in the whirlwind.
Do they not call tornados,
hurricanes, typhoons, tsunamis
acts of God? Yet, listen to his still,
small voice in whispers of snow.

Enter into the Holy of Holies.
Enter into the sacred space
of your mind in hushed silence.
Listen to the Holy Spirit unction.
Long for the Logos; Rhema will come.

Pursue God as the Quakers,
sitting quietly for the Light
of our Lord to shine within.
Delve deeper into sanctuary
until your temple shakes with
Holy Ghost charisma,
and Upper Room tongues.

Seek not visions.
If they come, so be it.
Let the vision of faith
lead into magnificence
beyond your imagination
of the power of the omnipotent
and omnipresent Almighty God.

Cornelius and Peter's Visions and Missions

(Villanelle)

An angel appeared in a vision
when a Roman centurion prayed.
The Gentile sent men on a mission.

Peter, a Jew with circumcision
laws, prayed and fasted on his face. Lay
prone before God until a vision

rebuked Peter about division
between Jews and Gentiles. He raved
"Are the unclean also my mission?"

Peter overcame opposition
when God made pure the unclean. Pete caved,
trading law for grace. Trust the vision.

Gentiles came without suspicion
and pleaded Peter go the way paved
by angel visions for God's mission.

Jew and Gentile, quit derision.
Cornelius's kin by grace were saved.
Because each man obeyed God' visions
and altered their ideas of mission.

Gold Vials of Prayers

Our Father—

First holy exhalation
of carbon monoxide
chemically transforms
to *ketoret*, incense offerings

in heaven—

to the very throne room
in the utmost, highest
heavenly realm,
pearly gate, jasper prayer wall.

hallowed be your name—

Praising, pleading, petitioning
The Holy, Almighty, Yahweh,
Alpha and Omega, Redeemer,
all-encompassing I Am.

Your kingdom come—

We, saints, await in prayer
for Christ's Second Coming,
await with twenty-four elders.
Seraphim cry, "Holy, holy, holy."

Your will be done—

Elders uncork gold vials.
Sweet savor smoke arises,
piercing the stratosphere
with crux of our prayers.

On earth as it is in heaven—

Dare we hope? You have
already given us your Son,
your Holy Spirit. Adjoining
us with a royal promise.

Give us this day our daily bread—

And yet we grouse for quail,
complain manna is not enough.
Leftover rot decays, fouling
the air, masking the incense.

Forgive us our debts—

Cover our transgressions,
debts we cannot repay.
Redeeming mercy and grace
by the blood of our Lamb.

As we forgive our debtors—

With lying lips we offend.
With tongues we apologize.
Our mouths offer contrition.
Fragrant offerings of words.

Do not lead us into temptation—

In our weak volition we violate
your laws of godliness. The stench
of sin offends your nostrils.
Deliver us from crooked paths.

Deliver us from the evil one—

Who reeks of sulfur from dwelling
in the fire-stoked bowels of hell.
Deliver us from the Adamic curse.
Accept offerings of prayer and praise.

For yours is the kingdom and power and glory forever.

Prayers of the saints, as sweet
smelling aroma, fills gold vials.
Elders cork and seal the bottles.
Pick up golden harps and sing.

Amen.

The Maid

Wind, a frigid sword.
Earth, hard as iron.
Sun shuttered
behind wintery clouds.
Yet, I am warmed within
by the light of my Lord.

It always begins with the light
surrounding me like the Holy
of Holies in my Father's temple.
The light comes before the voices.
Voices so clear and near
as angels and saints speak to me.

The inquisitors ask about the voice.
Yet, how can I describe the visitations
to those who do not see, do not hear?
Though the spirits come to Christians
who will not yield to Christ in sight,
refuse to listen to what God says.

I am but a peasant handmaiden,
devoted to my Abba Father
and his son Jesus Christ.
At thirteen I yielded my body,
promising to remain pure,
in devotion to my Lord.

Light engulfed me
in a warm embrace.
Voices spoke to me
in firm commands.
Troubling, for who am I
but a simple maid?

The bishop demands again and again,
accusing me of heresy and whoredom.
Yet, there are no earthly words
in any language to adequately describe
mysteries of the spirit. Visions
and voices, so clear and strong.

A mist of vapor within a fog,
we look through a glass darkly.
Yet, I cannot express to satisfaction
to those who do not see at all.
To those who choose not to listen.
I only know what I have seen and heard.

Believing with all my heart
the voices are from God.
The commands are from God
The battle strategies are from God.
My devotion is to my country and king.
My ultimate allegiance is to my Lord.

Though I be imprisoned,
falsely accused of heresy,
condemned of witchcraft,
and burned at the stake,
I refuse to denounce the voices
of angels and saints.

I am but a maid
in obedience to Christ.

The Trumpet Sounds

Listen.
Listen!
Listen for the voice.
Not any voice.
Not the voice of peers
or deceivers.
Listen for the voice
of the Archangel
Gabriel, chief in God's army.
The holy sanctified voice
of God, calling from heaven.

Listen.
Listen!
Listen for the trumpet.
Not a flute.
Not a drum,
nor cello.
Listen for the cornet,
in the key of B-flat.
A piercing clarion blast,
sounding not a call to arms,
but calling us to join our Lord

in the air. Together,
dead and living—
holy, righteous, blood-bought
saints. Arise. Arise!
Those who heed the call.
Those who hear the voice.
Those who hear the trumpet.
Arise!
We shall be changed in an eye's
twinkle. We shall join Christ
with Holy God for eternity.

Listen. For it is with a sound
we shall hear
the voice and horn
of heaven.
Calling, calling
us home.

Four Horseman of the Apocalypse

"Who is worthy to open the book?"
an angel's voice rumbles.
No one on earth or in heaven
proves blameless before God.
Great trembling and tears
quakes at the knowledge
none are worthy. No not one,
save the spotless Lamb.
A holy hush falls as the Good
Shepherd takes the book.

The mighty Messiah, both lion and lamb,
slides his finger of his nail-pierced hand
under the first wax seal, opens the book.

A seraph's wings flap faster,
sounding like a helicopter landing.
"Holy, holy, holy! Lord God almighty!"
Thundering hoofbeats of a white horse
drowns out the beast's roaring voice.
Gallop, gallop, gallop… The rider clutches
an archery bow. A crown shows authority
and power. The archer rides off on the white
stallion of the apocalypse to conquer nations.

Plumes of dust rise in the thermosphere
when the Lamb who was slain for mankind
presses his fingernail through the second seal.
As it opens, heaven and earth shakes. Lightning
flashes, and a red horse *gallop, gallop gallops.*
A laurel wreath encircles the little horn on
the horseman's head. He unsheathes Goliath's
sword and charges with a clap of thunder,
intent on setting neighbor against neighbor.
Greatest slaughter the world has never known.

The white and red horsemen,
abomination and desolation,
set in motion all pain to come.
Torment of flesh and soul
fells the spirit to its knees.

An angel hands the Lamb a third seal.
Again, he slips his finger under the wax.
Has mankind not suffered enough?
They had their chance to make a choice.
They chose malice, hatred, and division.
What gallops next is a sweaty black horse,
unbalanced scales in the horseman's hands.
Famine devours on the heels of war.
Fallow fields. Drought-parched earth.
Costs too high for food; the price of war
exorbitant to save humanity from starvation
as the black horseman thirsts for blood.

The fourth seal of the apocalypse
lay in the King's hand. As the Lamb
reaches for it – does he hesitate?
(Or did John the Revelator blink?)—
Another seal opens. Hoofbeats
roar. Seemingly rising from a cloud,
a horse so pale it appears translucent.
A horse so pale and ghostly, it
gallop, gallop, gallops throughout
a fourth of Earth. "My name is Death."
The pale horse rears up, turns swiftly,
and charges down the corridor of Hell.

Thus are the visions of the first four seals
showing John on the Isle of Patmos
the Four Horseman of the Apocalypse.

Elegy to the Martyrs

I, John, while exiled on the Isle of Patmos
laid in a trance; God showed me a vision.

Visions of horror—Four Horseman
of Apocalypse caused war, famine,
death to reign upon the Earth.

I lifted my tear-filled eyes
with trepidation to the Lamb
holding the fifth seal.
What could be worse?

Jesus' eyes held mine. I knew
that look, sorrow and compassion.
My body clenched, bracing myself.
He unlocked the seal, eyes flicking
to the brazen altar. Incense billowed.

There, below the holy altar of God,
stood my older brother. "James!"
I cried, bolting upright and holding
out my arms, longing to touch him.

Beside James—(they called us Sons
of Thunder. The memory almost
brings a smile)—stood Peter, Andrew,
Bartholomew and Thomas. Fog
lifted from my brain and the dawn
of understanding filled me with grief.
In anguish I fell prostrate before God.

These were the martyred saints,
my brothers in Christ, the disciples
slain. Through clouded eyes I blinked,
looked again. Ah, yes. John the Baptist
huddled with them. Elder Stephen
and Paul, once an enemy of the cross,
shoulder to shoulder, friends in death.

My heart weighed heavy with grief.
They cried in unity, "Who will avenge
our blood? How long until judgement?
The King handed each disciple,
including my beloved brother,
a white robe and said, "Wait
for a season of justice to rule.
Then peace on Earth forever."

I collapsed in fresh mourning,
and watched for the sixth seal.

No End or Beginning

Open the Book.
Come. See. Read for yourself.
Revelation, Genesis,
reflections in a mirror.
Omega, Alpha,
cyclical nature of God
who has no end or beginning.

In the beginning God created
Heaven, then Earth.
In the ending God re-creates
Heaven and Earth.
God formed moon and sun.
In the ending, God's glory
shines eternally with no need
for blood moons and great
balls of fire (except in hell.)

Come. Taste. Sweet juicy
roll-down-your elbow fruit.
Twelve types, pick your own
fruit of the month garden club.
Tree of Life public park.
Eden's cherub reassigned.
Mirror images, cyclical seasons.

Come. Drink. Never thirst.
A river of water flows from
the King of king's throne.
Water sparkling as the Tigris,
Euphrates in the Garden of Eden,
immaculately, conceptually restored
in New Heaven and New Earth
reflected, refracted in Revelation
from Genesis. All things made new.

Come. Feel. Let God dry your tears.
No sorrow. No sickness. No death.
Eden restored. Without the wily
serpent, the archangel Satan, who is
thrown in the lake of fire, brimstone.
Immanuel. In communion.
In fellowship. He walks and talks
with us. Again. God dwells with us.
Forever and ever and ever. Amen.

www.ingramcontent.com/pod-product-compliance
Lightning Source LLC
Chambersburg PA
CBHW071732040426
42446CB00011B/2327